# HOW TO GET OUT OF DEBT

AND LIVE A FINANCIALLY HEALTHY LIFE

## 6 SIMPLE STEPS

# Contents

# About This Book

A re you trapped in debt and can't figure out how, when, or whether you'll ever set yourself free? Are you looking for ways of earning extra income and putting an end to your financial struggles and frustrations? Or do you just long to take proper charge of your finances and live a financially healthy and fulfilling life?

If you are seeking answers to such questions then this book is your perfect read. It has no hidden secrets, tricks, shortcuts, or even visualization exercises. If you believe you can manifest your way out of debt and experience a financially healthy life simply by thinking about it, then you should put this book a side and spend as much time as you can doing just that! Don't you think it's worth the effort? Instead, this book presents practical things you can do to take personal responsibility for getting out of debt, and goes on to offer you invaluable money tricks to help you live a truly relaxed and financially healthy life.

Read this book if you want to build something beautiful on the road towards your financial freedom.

# Demystifying The Three Notorious Myths About Debt

B eing trapped in debt can be a stressful ordeal to subject yourself through! The moment you've accessed credit from lenders or creditors, you are legally duty-bound to pay it back, regardless of any bad luck that might befall you (such as loss of your job, or even falling sick).

Most probably, you've heard these three notorious myths about debt which are being peddled by a number of people trapped in debt. But it's time to separate the precious wheat from the unhealthy chaff.

**First myth:** One only gets into debt because of meager earnings.

**Truth:** It's never how much you earn or how early/how late you receive your earnings which determine how likely you get trapped in debt! It's your financial lifestyle; how you put into use that which you earn, which determines your level of financial success.

**Second myth:** Having a huge debt gives you immunity against job termination at the workplace.

**Truth:** Well, I think this is madness! Your inability to honor payments of your debts can hinder your concentration both at home and at the workplace. You'll be forced to focus much of your time trying to figure out possible solutions for your debt predicament. And which employer do you think has time for an unfocussed employee in a world littered with job seekers?

**Third myth:** If the credit is offered at a low interest, take it, as fast as you can, even if you have no any pre-planned use of that money.

**Truth:** You are literally testing the depth of an ocean with both of your feet! However small the interest on that credit is, always remember that it is a debt which must eventually be paid back. It's never free money!

## (Step One)

## If It Has To Be, Then It's Up To You

Borrowing more, even at high interest rates to pay out existing debts, and trying to run or hide from the lenders and creditors can make you a permanent slave of debt

**H**ave you heard of the popular quote *'if it has to be, then it's up to you'*? Fact is, keeping your eyes closed in a burning house doesn't help extinguish the fire! Instead, when you eventually open them up, you shall have lost direction and most probably, end up consumed in the burning flames! Therefore, you've got to act swiftly to contain that fire, or let it consume you.

When trapped in debt, the first step towards setting yourself free is to acknowledge that you are in a fix, and in need of help. You must never wait for your employer, spouse, sister, brother, cousin, friend, or any other relation to push you towards re-aligning your financial off-track back to track. You must be honest with yourself, acknowledge that you are in need of help, and go get that help.

Be bold enough and face the situation head on. Trying to run away or hide is a game you'll seldom win. And if you sit back and do nothing, then the debts will most probably outgrow your income, and consequently subject you to endless financial humiliations.

Debt can be effectively managed, don't let it destroy your life! But you must be the one to make that bold move towards turning things around. You must step up and acknowledge that enough is enough. You've got to make a decision to stop living from debts, from one paycheck to the next, or from relying on merger earnings and chose to take the path of financial abundance.

You should never allow lenders and creditors to turn your paycheck into their shopping mall, each one fighting for a

> Never allow lenders and creditors to turn your paycheck into their shopping mall, each one fighting for a space to deduct the limited money you earn

space to deduct the limited money you earn. Well, it's undeniable that the offers from most lenders will always be tempting, but you should manage your appetite and avoid taking unnecessary loans to block them from scavenging for a space on your precious paycheck.

When trapped in debt, the process of getting back on your feet might seem physically overwhelming, but you must persistently hold on to a proven debt exit plan in order to realize plausible results. You need to prepare yourself together with your household, both physically and emotionally, for the uncomfortable journey a head.

> You would rather spend five years struggling financially, but thereafter, enjoy financial abundance for the rest of your life

You would rather spend five years struggling financially, but thereafter, enjoy financial abundance for the rest of your life!

The clouds can hide the sun for a while, but not forever. Notably, the clouds can never replace the sun. Living a financially healthy life should be your sun, and the debts trying to pull you down should just be temporary dark clouds trying to block your sun's rays.

If it has to be, then it's up to you. You are never going to miraculously revive your predicament without any effort! The journey towards getting out of debt is one that not all who embark on successfully accomplish. It's a journey not for the faint at heart! But the good news is, once you effectively commit to getting back on your feet, no matter how long it takes, you'll eventually be back on your feet and sparkle again, financially.

(Step Two)

# Find Some Quite Space

The moment you've decided to put an end to your debt predicament, find some quiet space, sit down with a copy of your paycheck (if any), then identify and capture all the details of exactly how much you owe, to whom, at what rates, and for how long

**B**eing engulfed in unending debt can not only give you sleepless nights, it can destroy your life, and possibly kill you! Many people are ensnared into debt from all the good and bad sources such as excessive spending (overspending), borrowing to spend on emergencies, loss of source of income such as employment, development reasons such as building a house or purchasing a piece of land, payment of school fees, and even from bad habits such as gambling, drug and alcohol abuse etc.

So, you are not alone! Today, the number of people trapped in debt is as ubiquitous as the many lenders and creditors that continue to open shop everywhere, day in day out. And the sad truth is, debt is fun to acquire, but it takes blood and sweat to pay it back. And there is never something like *free money* from the lenders or creditors. You can't even get such *free money* from lotteries since you must first purchase relevant tickets!

The moment you've decided to put an end to your debt predicament, you need to find some quiet space, and sit down with a copy of your paycheck (if any), then identify and capture all the details of exactly how much you owe, to whom, at what rates, and for how long. Clearly capture the amounts of car loan, personal loan, credit card, mortgage, student loan, loans from shylocks etc you owe, to which creditor/lender, at what rate, and for how long. Without writing down these exact details and figures down, it would be difficult to acknowledge that you are indeed in debt.

Afterwards, identify the circumstances that drove you into acquiring each debt. Was it an emergency, a necessity, a want, or you got into that debt for the fun of it? You need to clearly establish the root cause of your debt predicament because if you don't know where you are coming from, it would be difficult to set up your direction, and thus your destination. If you don't know what got you into that debt, paying it up would only pave a smooth way for you to run back into acquiring more of it.

Once you've identified the circumstances that drove you into acquiring each debt, classify them into two groups; **the good ones**, and **the bad ones**. If you borrowed money to purchase a house, a piece of land, or to pay school fees (or to acquire assets with appreciating values), then such would fall under the good ones. But if you borrowed money to purchase lifestyle-related items that you could have comfortably saved for, or borrowed to utilize on bad habits such as gambling, (or wasted the money on liabilities with depreciating values) then such would fall under the bad ones.

And moving forward, you must shun all the habits that drove you into acquiring the debts you've grouped under the bad ones, if you want to realize healthy results.

Just because your paycheck has a space to accommodate a loan deduction doesn't mean you should commit that deduction towards paying installments for items you can comfortably save for, such as a new TV, a new top notch music system, a new classy furniture, organizing a costly party, or going for an unplanned holiday. Such would be an outright abuse of that credit.

> Just because your paycheck has a space to accommodate a loan deduction doesn't mean you should commit that deduction towards paying installments for items you can comfortably save for

And do you know some of the most common traps that lure most people into debt? Take a look at the **below seven most common debt traps.**

1.  **Taking more loans to pay out other loans**

    One grave mistake committed by a number of people engulfed in debt is trying to take more loans, from different lenders; even with higher interest rates, to pay out other debts. You'll seldom get out of that debt trap if you decide to take this route.

2.  **Unplanned debt consolidation**

    Others take one major loan in pursuit of paying off other smaller loans. In most cases, such huge loans are usually given for an extended period of time. In the long run, they end up paying the major loan for a longer duration of time, and sometimes at a higher interest rate.

3.  **Topping up existing loans**

    Lenders and creditors will always encourage you to 'top up' your existing loans with slightly higher amounts, and at sometimes slightly higher interest rates. A typical example is borrowing a five year loan to purchase say household electronics. After diligently paying the credit for say two and half years, you are lured by the lender to top-up the loan and use the little amount on top to purchase other personal stuff with non-increasing values. This is a common trap many people find themselves in.

They keep on topping up their existing loans to the point that they carry the loan burden into their retirement!

## 4. Unplanned borrowing

The fact that you qualify for a loan or have an easy or quick access to a credit facility should not be an excuse for you to take it if you have no planned use for it. Equally, you do not necessarily need to borrow money simply because you've seen your colleague or friend do so. This is a common debt trap that many people walk into with their eyes wide open.

## 5. Investing more in liabilities than in assets

If you buy land today, in five year's time, its value shall have increased. But if you buy a personal car today, in five year's time, its value shall have depreciated, and you shall have spent an almost similar amount of its buying price to maintain it. Unlike assets, liabilities usually have no or minimal returns. Consequently, borrowing to spend on more liabilities than on assets often traps people in unending debt.

## 6. That wedding loan

Some people are lured into borrowing money to help them organize a memorable wedding. However, any successful wedding should not propel the newlyweds into spending the rest of their married lives in debt. A number of new couples have had their beautiful marriage dreams short lived because they either knowingly or unknowingly lured themselves into that wedding debt; but none of them is now willing to take full responsibility of paying that loan. And this is further complicated if already there are children in the marriage.

7. **That holiday loan**

Borrowing money to go for a holiday is an outright abuse of that credit.

# (Step Three)

# Involve Your Household

**Fighting debt as a team (as a household) usually yields greater and faster results than doing so individually.**

Closing your eyes when it's raining can never stop the rain. Equally, however long the clouds can struggle to hide the sun, it doesn't mean that there is no sun.

Instead of waking up the next morning and issuing an executive order; cutting on all major family's expenses, call your household to a meeting, then open up and clearly state to them the need of re-looking into family's expenditure and adjusting it accordingly.

Truth is, involving the members of your family will definitely get you greater and faster results. If young children are part of the household, call them to the meeting as well, but you can spare them all the finer details of the debt(s). However, you have a duty to make then understand why the changes you are suggesting are vital.

Did you know that involving young children in deciding on which items to cut back on exposes them at such a tender age to knowing the difference between the vital basic human needs and the sometimes not-so-necessary human desires.

As already stated, fighting debt as a team (as a household) usually yields greater and faster results than doing so individually. And do you know how you and your household leak money, day in day out? **Here below are the eighteen most common ways**

1. **Impulse buying**

   You just walk into a supermarket and start purchasing items simply because its payday and you have money in abundance. When you reach home, you realize that you've purchased more of the items you don't need than those you are in dire need of. And what's the disclaimer on that purchase receipt? *'Goods once sold cannot be returned or exchanged'*

2. **Purchasing more goods or services outside your budgetary allocation**

Also commonly referred to as excessive spending, this is one of the leading causes of money leak! And on a lighter note, you should note that even governments are run on budgets.

3. **Spending just to please others**

I prefer terming this as unsolicited philanthropy. It may also be in the form of spending out of peer influence. You decide to spend your hard earned money on unworthy items or services just to make you not fall out of place with your peers.

4. **Spending beyond your means**

Your mode of transport, where you live and what you eat should always be in alignment with your income if you yearn to live a financially stress-free life.

5. **Emotional-driven spending**

Spending out of rage, past disappointment, or simply to prove someone wrong. In most cases, this pushes the affected persons into buying more of liabilities than assets.

6. **Spending on wrong investments**

Those that are hurriedly done without the input of trained/experienced investment professionals. They always backfire and eventually make you waste a lot of money!

7. **The 'mentor influence'**

Spending on goods and services that your 'mentor' or someone you look up to maybe in possession of i.e. a new trendy cloth or a sleek car (without giving due consideration to your purchasing power). You then rush to borrow money and after a few months, that item becomes out of fashion. You again shop for the next trendy item in the market? Such will always make you leak endless amount of money.

8. **Delegating your spending responsibility**

You send other people to purchase for you goods and services though you have time and even means of transport to realize this. You then end up paying unclear prices and even compensating the person you have sent with avoidable monetary or non monetary rewards.

9. **Abusing debit and credit cards**

Withdrawing small sums of cash at the automated teller machines (ATMs) on a regular basis. You end up paying more on the withdrawal charges. Equally, withdrawing money at alternative money providers charging higher service rates exposes you to paying more charges at the end of the day. Equally, exhausting the limit on your credit card makes you pay higher interest charges, hence leaking your money.

## 10. **Speed spending**

A number of people, especially men, are always in a hurry to spend their money in a hurry, without giving due regard to value or the true price of the items or services they are purchasing. They eventually end up paying more or buying items or getting services of lower quality and at inflated prices.

## 11. **Paying bribe**

Hiding in the name of 'a thank you tip', to secure services you truly deserve. Well, to offer a tip is human, but to offer a 'tip' with a left hand and expecting your 'purchase' with a right hand is an outright abuse of that 'tip'. And it's more worse if the 'tip' involved is money.

## 12. **The 'gift curse'**

Unending urge to give out your hard earned valuable assets freely as gifts, even unto people who will never appreciate your reward.

## 13. **Over celebration**

This could be due to some great achievement, but done beyond your means of income.

## 14. Spending on avoidable emergencies

Spending on sudden natural and or un-natural emergencies which sometimes may be within one's control i.e. sudden loss of job or sickness. One ought to be prepared for such rainy days by taking an investment or an insurance cover. Have an emergency kitty where you can access money for such emergencies.

## 15. Abusing phone credit

The emergence of smart phones has give rise to endless mobile phone applications which heavily rely on internet to function. And even to access the social sites such as twitter, Facebook, Whatsapp, Instagram etc via these smart phones, you must have a functioning internet connection. But instead of purchasing internet bundles, or connecting to some free Wifi hotspot, most people rely on their phone's airtime; which is expensive in the long run. Also, continuous borrowing of phone credit makes you incur extra expenses, especially if the credit is offered at a fee.

## 16. Those little things you don't take serious in the house

Non use of energy saving bulbs, non switching of electric gadgets not in use, lack of knowledge of basic prices of items, leaving money in the pockets of dirty clothes you are giving out for washing etc. These are avenues for money leaks.

17. **Late payments of loans**

Generally, late payments of credit facilities usually attract penalties from the lenders and creditors in the form of increased interest payment on that loan.

18. **Opting to pay interest on a borrowed loan for a longer duration of time, instead of paying part of the principal, or even all of it**

Whether the loan amount is small or big, opting to pay just the interest, and not the full loan or part of it, is always an expensive undertaking in the long run.

(Step Four)

# Start By Building An Emergency Kitty

**D**id you know that lack of an emergency kitty will often force you to view credit as your sole safety net? It's advisable to have an emergency kitty of at least $1500 if you truly want peace of mind as you go about repaying debts. This fund will be your water-tight buffer between you and the debts.

To be able to build up an emergency kitty as fast as possible, pay up your debts in the shortest time possible, and have surplus money at your disposal, you need to find creative ways of making extra money without turning to credit.

Well, today, there are endless things you can do to make extra money. Here below are the **twenty six things you can do to make more money**

1. **Take and sell photos online**

   Websites such as iStock iStock, Fotolia, Shutterstock, and Photoshelter offers opportunities for anyone with a great photo to earn some income by selling it.

   If you have a smartphone with good photo features, or any camera capable of taking great photos, then you can utilize such for profitable use.

2. **Hire out your car, boat, motorbike or bicycle**

   If you have any of these, you can hire them out to close friends, family, or neighbors at a fee.

   You can also link up with Taxi services providers such as Uber and use their platform to access clients or even to offer your driver-services (if you qualify).

3. **Do you have a skill you can trade for $5?**

   If your answer is yes then head to Fiverr.com , create a profile and offer it. Fiverr.com offers a virtual marketplace where people sell and buy services from as low as $5.

Are you a graphic designer? Can you edit documents? Can you produce short videos or audios? Can you write or review articles? Can you review books, songs or products? You have all these options and many more available at Fiverr.com. The beauty of using this platform is that you can complete a number offers in a couple of minutes and move on to others. And it's what you can do and the time you are willing to put into it which determines how much you take home at the end of the day.

4. **Run errands for other people**

If you have means of transport, you can run errands for other people. Your friends, colleagues, or neighbors may be looking for someone to help them move to a new house/home or to assist them pick up some items from the local store. Watch out for such opportunities and grab them. You can also advertise your services on social media platforms such as local Facebook groups and through Thumbtack.

5. **Create and monetize a blog or website**

Are you an expert in a certain field or subject? Do you have a unique story or experience you would love to share with others? Create a blog or a website and monetize it (put Google Ads or Google affiliate ads such as Infolinks or Chitika adds on that blog/website to earn you some extra income). A number of people have ended up quitting their well paying jobs to concentrate on building their blogs or websites due to massive income they generate from the ads placed on those sites. Don't you think it's a cool way to boost your income?

6. **Charge some fee to take professional photos or play music at weddings or events**

If you can take those professional photos, you can consider charging some fee to do so. If you can also play music instruments such as a violin or have DJ skills, you can also consider advertising your skills for events on social platforms or through sites such as Craigslist, Thumbtack., gigmasters.com, weddingwire.com, and gigsalad.com.

7. **Take up mystery shopping assignments**

If you can spare some time, then you can consider picking up a mystery shopping gig, and provide feedback to the provider. To access a number of scam-free mystery shopping tasks, visit the Mystery Shopping Providers Association.

8. **Sell items you don't use**

You can assemble items you no longer use at home or those that you don't find good use of and sell them on

Sell and Buy platforms such as *Olx, local Facebook Sell and Buy Groups, Craigslist, EBay* etc.

Those old electronics, used text books, oversized or undersized clothes and many more. The maximum amount of money you can raise from doing this depends on the value and quantity of the items you are selling, and the effort you'll be putting towards realizing success.

9. **Find avenues of earning more income from your current job**

If you are in a commission based job, then this is the time to work extra hard, or extra smart and earn more commissions through provided earning channels. And if there is an opportunity for overtime payment then you should utilize it towards earning more.

10. **Find a better paying job:**

If the nature of your job is kind of fixed on a certain salary scale, then you can consider looking for a secondary job or a part time job elsewhere (as long as it doesn't conflict with your current job) to help you boost your income. This might sound unconventional, but truth is, you are not going to work all your life. If you believe you are not being paid according to the kind of work you do and the value you bring to that organization, then you should consider looking for a better paying job elsewhere. However, you should do this professionally. This would not only boost your current income, but also your lifetime earnings. And in case your employer might be unwilling to let you go, then you can consider negotiating for a pay rise.

11. **Reduce your expenses**

Reducing your expenses doesn't mean that you are now resorting to living a cheap life. It means cutting back on those excesses in your spending. It means lowering your wastage. If you eat out often, then this is the time to make adjustments and start eating at home, or carry packed food to work place. That TV subscription you rarely use, or that monthly membership subscription to a yoga class you rarely attend can take a back seat for a while .Find what to cut back on to help you save some money.

12. **Can you spare some time to take surveys and read mails?**

Many websites offer platforms where you are paid to take certain short surveys, listen to certain songs for a short duration of time, or read some short-worded emails. A good example is Inbox Dollars. You'll join for free and you get $5 just for signing up. And once your earnings reach stipulated amount, then you can withdraw your earnings through requesting for a check or receive it through your PayPal account. And once you sign up with them, you'll continue getting other unending offers from other websites linked to them. You can also check SwagBucks.

### 13. **Become a translator**

If you are gifted with a spare language (bilingual or multilingual), you can consider doing part time translation work. Check Translatorstown, Peopleperhour, iWriter, Freelancer, Gengo, UpWork or Guru if you can find some translation assignment. You can also advertise your services on social media sites to help access more clients.

### 14. **Find some freelancing work**

If you have problem solving skills or you are a people person, you can consider pursuing a customer service or a virtual assistant freelancing work on sites such as *Craigslist*, VirtualAssistants.com, **Fiverr**, Freelancer, UpWork, Guru and even on Zirtual.

And if you can write academic or business articles, you can pick up assignments on iWriter, Peopleperhour, Freelancer, UpWork or Guru. Depending on your skill and effort, Freelancing offers opportunities for unlimited rewards. If you are skilled in design work, you can bid for jobs at sites such as 99Designs.com.

### 15. **Don't ignore those sweepstakes and opportunities to enter raffle draws**

As proverbially connoted, you never know what you can achieve until you try. But do this responsibly. Don't insist on stopping only if you win the jackpot. Know when to pause, and when to eventually stop.

16. **Can you spare your home or some room within your home/house**

Many people make good money by renting out their homes or a room within their homes to tourists or travelers. You can access potential clients through sites such as vrbo.com, Expedia.com, airbnb.com, Jumuia travel, booking.com, roomorama.com, and Trip Advisor.

17. **Take up a tutor job**

Are you skilled in a particular subject or topic. You can charge a fee to tutor students or even adults within your locality. You can also find tutor related assignments on sites such as Chegg Tutors, and Tutor.com.. Equally, you can also consider teaching online courses via sites such as as Chegg Tutors teach.udemy.com, studypool.com, or Skillshare.

18. **Raise money through crowd funding**

There are several crowd funding platforms you can utilize to raise money towards funding your dream ideas, or for any other cause. Kickstarter, Indiegogo, GoFundMe, Crowdfunder, Crowdsupply and YouCaring are just a few examples of such sites. The trick in raising money through Crowd funding is to write a compelling message that would lure people to donate towards your cause.

19. **Join a focus group**

Focus group platforms such as focusgroup.com, mysurvey.com,harrispollonline.com,focuspointeglobal.co m, ipoll.com, inspiredopinions.com and swagbucks.com lists available opportunities in select areas, and equally pays you to complete certain surveys. Typically, focus groups rely on select participants to solicit for feedback on products and services offered by various brands, organizations, and businesses. This is vital in market research for the involved entities.

## 20. Sit or walk pets

You can do this on a part time or full time engagement. You can equally consider taking daytime or night time offers. Notably, you can find offers on platforms such as *Craigslist*, Care.com, and dogvacay.com.

## 21. Coach others at a fee

Do you have an experience or skill in Yoga? Can you mentor others in areas such as public speaking? Are you experienced in advanced computer packages such as Excel, Spss or Stata? Can you train others on how to skate or how to play any game? Then find interested parties and coach them at a fee. You can create a website or advertise your services through social media sites.

## 22. Make money from your craft

Can you make those unique handmade items? Can you make jewelry, or knit unique items? Can you draw or curve portraits? What unique craft do you have that you can sell to others? Use websites such as etsy.com or craftcoxes.com to access clients and sell such crafts.

23. **Be an independent tour guide**

Can you devote some time to give tourists or travelers and in-depth tour guide around your locality, town, city or country? You can market your services on social media platforms and on websites such as vayable.com.

24. **Buy select items at wholesale prices (discounted prices) and sell them for profit**

You can buy toys at wholesale prices and sell them at kids' events. Equally, you can buy bottled water at wholesale prices and sell them at events such as a friend's wedding or at local parties. Just find any item which has proven selling potential, get it at wholesale price (discounted price) and then sell it at a profitable retail price.

25. **Earn from Media ads**

Is your home close to main road or highway? You can rent a space on the wall of your house for an erection of a media billboard at a cost. Equally, you can allow ads to be placed on your car at a cost. Check examples at freecarmedia.com. If you feel you look gorgeous, you can consider modeling on part time or full time basis.

26. **Can you risk being a guinea pig?**

Can you risk being used in a clinical trial in exchange for some good amount of money? Then you can check for available offers from sites such as clinicaltrials.gov

**N/B:** Some of the suggested ways might not offer you the *get-it-quick* or so much money, but at least they offer you avenues of making extra money in a more relaxed and fun way.

(Step Five)

# Organize The Debts And Start Paying Them

There are several strategies you can utilize to organize the debts and begin your repayment. Here are **three most common effective strategies for organizing and repaying debts**

1. **Arrange all the debts with the ones charging high interest rates top on the list, and downwards (closing the list with the one charging lowest interest rate).**

   You first identify the debt attracting the highest interest rate, and then channel all your repayments towards clearing it. Once fully paid, you then use the installment which was going to it, add it to the installment going to the second debt with the second highest interest rate. Once fully paid, you'll then use the installments which were going to the first and second debts towards payment of installments for the third loan, and this goes on until you clear up all the loans.

The beauty of utilizing this strategy is that it allows you to save more money. The mathematics behind it is that if you were to pay a debt attracting a higher interest rate for a longer duration of time, then you would end up paying more interest on that debt. Paying the same debt on a shorter duration attracts less interest payment.

2. **Arrange the debts in a descending manner (with those having highest balances top on the list, and the ones with lowest balances down the list).**

With this approach, you identify the debt with the highest balance, and then channel all your repayments towards clearing it. Once fully paid off, you then use the installment which was going to it, add it to the installment going to the second debt with the second highest balance. Once fully paid, you then use the installments which were going to the first and second debts towards payment of installments for the third loan, and this goes on until you clear up all the loans.

This strategy is more useful if you have gotten some good amount of extra money (say from some bonus payment) and you would wish to throw it at the debts. Once you clear the loan with the highest balance, you'll gain some confidence and momentum towards clearing the second one, the third one ...and all the remaining ones.

3. **You can arrange the debts in ascending manner (with those having lowest balances top on the list, and the ones with highest balances closing the list).**

Here, you will channel all your repayments towards clearing that debt with the lowest balance first. Once fully paid off, you then add the installment which was going towards it to the installment going to the second debt with the second lowest balance. Once also fully paid, you then use the installments which were going to the first and second debts towards payment of installments for the third loan, and this goes on until you clear up all the loans.

This strategy is equally vital if you are looking for motivation and momentum towards clearing the debts.

If any of your debts are being repaid through a check-off system via your employer, in most cases, you would not have the authority to stop any deduction going towards repayment of any loan and channel it towards paying another loan. What you can do in such a scenario is to utilize any extra money you have and throw it at any debt repayment strategy you've considered.

However, regardless of which debt-repaying strategy you decide to utilize, the most important thing is persisting with it to the end. It won't be easy, and that's why you must persist to realize plausible results.

Other than using the extra money you have made to pay up the debts, you can also rely on any of the below sources of funds:

**Four other sources of funds to help you pay debts**

- **Do you have any savings?**

    You can use part of your savings to help you offset part of the debts; especially those attracting high interest rates.

    To many, this might seem as an uncomfortable route, but if you deeply analyze the end results, you'll end up saving more on interests the debts would have accrued, as compared to the minimal interests that today's most savings accounts attracts.

    However, you should always take necessary precaution never to deplete all your savings towards debt repayment.

- **Have you received some windfall?**

    In case you've received some windfall (some good amount of money you didn't expect), use it to offset part of, or even all of your debts if it can allow. This will save you on paying part of the interest that your debt would have attracted if you were to continually pay the normal installments.

- **Use that bonus, or part of that hefty per diem to offset that debt**

While it might be tempting to pursue other projects or even to go for a holiday with that hefty bonus check from your employer, it would be wiser to use it to clear part of, or even all of your debts, if it can.

If you've received some hefty per diem, you can save part of that amount and use the remainder to offset part of, or all of that debt, if it can. Having your monthly debt repayment reduced by such a lump sum payment will hand you a more lighter debt to manage, and even reduce you repayment period. Instead of using that bonus money for short term gratifications such as going for a holiday, using it to offset your debt will hand you several years of financial freedom.

- **Perform a credit card balance transfer**

A credit card balance transfer is simply paying off a balance on one credit card by transferring it to another credit card. Using one credit card to pay off balance of another credit card; at a fee or for free. The trick here is to transfer the balances to credit cards that offer you zero or lesser interest rates. You can also get a balance transfer credit card ( a specially designed credit card to help you offset credit card balances at no, or at favorable costs).

(Step Six)

# 13 Financially Healthy And Highly Rewarding Habits You Should Consider Adopting

You were never born to merely exist and pay unending bills and debts. There is a lot of financial abundance in the world which you too, have a right to tap into and live a financially fulfilling life, just like many other people out there.

Here below are the **thirteen financially healthy and highly rewarding habits you should adopt** if you dream of living a financially healthy and rewarding life.

1.  **Live within your income**

    No amount of money will ever be enough to fully satisfy your day to day financial needs. Consequently, taking endless loans in pursuit of meeting your daily financial needs is a gamble you'll seldom win. In the end, you'll only get highly indebted and possibly, will never have peace of mind!

    You must learn to slow down on spending money you don't have and start running your befitting financial race. Live the life you can afford, within your income. Stay away from the temptation of borrowing money to spend on items you can comfortably purchase from your income/savings.

    Before you hurriedly embark on spending your hard-earned money on any item, here below are the four vital questions you must ask yourself to help cushion you against unnecessary or excessive spending.

    **The four vital questions you must ask yourself before spending money on any item**

    > **Question number One:** Is it necessary? - Can your life go on smoothly without purchasing that item /service?

**Question number Two:** How urgent do I need it? - What's the level of urgency involved? In other words, how bad do you want it?

**Question number Three:** Can I afford it? - In other words, can you comfortably acquire it without necessarily resorting to borrowing money elsewhere?

**Question number Four:** Will I be getting value for my money? - Is it original or counterfeit? How long is it expected to last? And is there any other seller offering a similar item at a lesser cost?

If it's necessary, it's urgent, you can afford it without borrowing money elsewhere, and you are getting value for your money, then that's a green light to make the purchase. But if you can't confidently answer all or at least three of the above questions, then that's a red light on that spending.

Always be contended with the things you can comfortably afford. Enjoy them and work hard to increase your income to enable you afford more. Your way of life should be a true reflection of your real income. Don't fake it or live a seemingly richer life that you can't comfortably sustain. Living within your income will help you thwart the urge of being lured into avoidable debt.

2. **Establish a secondary source of income, and even more**

The day you realize that no amount of money is enough is the day you finally graduate into adulthood. No amount of money is ever sufficient to completely quench the unending thirst of human financial needs. We all want more. We all desire to be in possession of all the beautiful things life can offer, yet these things are largely accessed financially.

The moment you establish your first source of income, finding a secondary source of income should be a priority. Even in the Bible, God established four rivers to water the blessed Garden of Eden. Why wouldn't He allow just one river to water the Garden? Wasn't Eden a blessed garden? You will always thrive in abundance when you rely on more than once source of income. And after securing the secondary source of income, work on the third, the fourth, the fifth, the sixth…….sources of income.

Have diverse sources of income. Never depend on one tributary, it might dry up sooner than you think and expose your world to drought!

3. **Budget for every coin you earn**

Except for emergencies, always budget for what you spend

your money on. I'm sure you've heard more than a thousand times the need of having a budget for every coin you earn. Why don't you commit putting this into action? Living without a budget is like trusting a toddler to successfully crawl across a busy highway. It's that risky!

Budgeting will help you keep track of your earnings vs. expenditure, and enable you put a right cap on your spending excesses. With budgeting, you'll stop viewing luxury living as some wish in a dreamland since you will always find some slots for your personal enjoyments, allowing you to gratify yourself as you go on with life. Having a right budget in place will always offer you a perfect escape route towards living a financially healthy lifestyle.

4. **Save and invest part of your earnings, that windfall, and that bonus**

It's never how much you have, how much you earn, or how early/late you receive your wages which determine your level of financial success in life. It's how you put into use that which you earn.

Truth is you are not going to work forever. Someday, you will be forced to leave the comfort of that business, or that office through old age, retirement, termination, resignation, or even on medical grounds (God forbid!) etc. You must therefore, learn to put your financial house in order before that bleak day arrives.

To live a financially secure and healthy life, you must effectively save and invest part of your earnings, that windfall, or that bonus. An age old tested savings principle is to save 10% of your net earnings, for a specific period of time, say five or ten years. Afterwards, you should carefully invest that saved amount somewhere safe where you'll earn a good interest.

When you invest money, you put it to work for you. As a result, it should be able to earn you a commensurate income. Significantly, you'll need to invest the money somewhere secure where you can access it whenever you desire to.

If you save and invest part of your earnings wisely, you shall have provided in advance for your future financial needs and those of your family. And even in your absence, the continuity of your family shall have been guaranteed financially.

To dig a little deep on savings and investments, let's me take you through some of **the most common terms used in the savings and investment world.**

- ✓ **Savings**: An amount of money kept aside, mostly in a financial institution such as a bank, possibly for future use. An amount of money not spent on current expenditures.

- ✓ **Income**: What you earn from your investment. Examples of income include coupons obtained from mature bonds, dividends payments from unit trusts/shares held, and interest earned from a fixed deposit account.

✓ **Risk**: Generally, risk is defined as a situation involving exposure to certain danger. All investments have certain elements of risk that an investor has to bear. Notably, there is an age-old financial maxim that *the greater the risk, the higher the expected rewards*. However, when investing your hard-earned money, you should keenly understand the risks involved in order to make an effective decision on whether to commit your money or not.

✓ **Investment horizon:** This is the amount of time you take to invest in order to realize your financial objectives.

✓ **Return on investment**: This is the gross gain or gross loss that you realize out of an investment. If say you invested in an item, then the return on that investment can either be a gain or loss in price of that item.

✓ **Net returns**: The total returns from your investment, less operational, administrative, and other related costs. It's the actual profit or loss after eliminating accompanying costs.

✓ **Capital gain/loss**: Simply the gain or loss that you make as a result of selling an asset/product at a price above/below the price you paid to acquire it.

**Factors you should consider before saving or investing any amount of money**

Below are some of the most vital factors to consider when faced with an investment option to settle on.

✓ **First, identify your investment goals with clarity**

What do you specifically want to achieve by saving or investing that money? Do you want it to grow, or do you just want it to be kept safe regardless of any expected profit? And how long are you willing to wait for it to mature?

✓ **Do you have an emergency fund?**

Before committing any amount of money towards savings or investment, ensure you have a cash reserve or a source of income capable of sustaining you throughout the period of the investment.

✓ **Understand the risks involved**

Are you capable of bearing the risks linked to your savings or investment? Are you able to move on in case you unfortunately lose all, or part of that money? Deciding to invest part or all of your money has accompanying rewards: negatives or positives. Are you able to live with the consequences of your decision to invest that money?

✓ **Carry out in depth research on other various savings and investment options available**

Don't settle on any savings or investment option with minimal rewards when the most rewarding and secure option is just a few minutes/hours/days of research away. Visit local financial institutions and insurance companies to explore various products that have the potential to offer you better returns on your investment.

✓ **Read in between the lines**

Go through the terms and conditions of the option you desire to settle on to establish what is on offer. Know what you'll gain by holding on to your investment till maturity, and what you may lose by an abrupt withdrawal of part or the entire amount. You will always have a peace of mind by investing in a product you have full knowledge of.

## ✓ Establish the cost of your investment

One true sad fact with most investment products from a number of financial institutions is that they have certain hidden costs which mostly, are never openly stated. Most clients only get to know about these hidden charges at the maturity of the invested amount, or when withdrawing the invested amount. Nonetheless, such costs (if any), are usually minimal and should not bar you from realizing your larger investment goals. It's therefore essential to always invest from a point of knowledge.

## ✓ Have plan B

What do you do when your sole investment option fails to live to your expectation? Do you just walk away heart-broken and vow never to invest any money again? Investments aren't matters of life and death. You may fail in one but succeed in another. The best investment strategy is to always find ways of spreading/minimizing the risks associated with your investment. If you have adequate cash, it's advisable to diversify your investments.

Below are some of the today's secure **savings and investments options you can consider**

❖ **Buying shares in the stock market**

Shares are generally issued by companies in bid to raise capital from investors. The moment you buy any company's share, you become its shareholder and are rightfully entitled to the company's share of any dividends it declares and pays out. Across the globe, people buy shares in hope that their prices will someday increase. Others buy them in pursuit of dividend payments, or as a shield against inflation.

Notably, listed companies pay dividends out of profits they make (if any). In certain instances, a listed company may decide to re-invest its profits into the business. And in the event the company is faced with liquidation but you still own part of its shares, then you are rightfully entitled to its remaining assets; but only after all its creditors have been settled.

When you own any company's shares, you have an option of selling them the moment the share price increases in value, or hold on to the share when prices are low.

Investing in shares is ideal for economic-savvy persons; people who can forecast the future performances/behaviors of the listed companies. However, with good advice from trustworthy stockbrokers or investment advisers, you can take a stab at buying the advised listed companies' shares.

There is an old-aged adage that *'you lose 100% of chances you fail to take.'* Most people are afraid of investing their money in the stock market. This has give room to a smaller portion of the population who are currently reaping heavy returns from various stock markets across the globe.

## ❖ Open a fixed deposit account

This is another exciting option offered by several financial institutions. They allow you to deposit/invest a specific amount of money at an agreed interest rate, for a specific duration of time.

This option is evidently better than merely opening a savings account since it has better returns on savings. However, you will be required to deposit your money for a specific period of time, without withdrawing any portion of it. In return, your money will yield some interest payable at the end of an agreed period.

You can consider putting your money in a fixed deposit account if you have no urgent/immediate use of it. And before putting your cash in any fixed deposit account, carefully go through the offer from the financial institution and ensure you properly understand the pros and cons of keeping your money with them. It's advisable to compare the offers from different financial institutions to get the best deal for your money.

## ❖ Invest in a structured deposit

A structured deposit has an investment option. It's different from a fixed deposit account since it offers potential for higher returns. But on the other hand, it has higher risks; such as receiving lower amounts than your expectation. The returns on structured deposits depend on the performance of assets/products which the money are invested in. Such may include shares, bonds, and other fixed income securities etc.

You will receive the principal amount you have invested in a structured deposit as long as you do not withdraw the money before maturity. If you leave it to maturity, you will be paid the principal amount and the agreed interest; provided the financial institution does not negate on the deal. Therefore, the credit risk of the financial institution holding your deposit is significant in helping you gauge the quality of your returns.

## ❖ Invest in bonds

A bond is form of borrowing. It's a debt security issued by a borrower i.e. a government or a company seeking to raise funds from the financial stock market(s).

A bond is classified as a fixed income security; it pays a steady flow of income at intervals throughout its life. Bonds are usually offered for a period of more than ten years (though there are certain instances where bonds may be offered for periods less than ten years). Other fixed income securities are Bills (debt securities maturing in less than one year), and Notes (debt securities maturing between one to ten years).

The life/duration of a bond is referred to as its tenure, and the interest from bonds are known as coupons. The rates of coupons are expressed as a percentage of the principal amounts, known as face values or par values. The prices of bonds are expressed as a % of the face value. Once a bond matures, it is redeemed at a face value, and those who hold the bonds are generally paid one hundred percent of the face value.

There are certain bonds which do not offer coupon payments at all. They are known as zero-coupon bonds. The prices of zero-coupon bonds are mostly discounted at the bonds' par values. I.e. a zero-coupon bond of say $10,000 par value is issued for 10 years at $7000. It means that you will be paying $7000 for a bond which will be worth $10,000 in ten years.

The prices of bonds are usually quoted as a percentage of the par value i.e. a bond of 110% or a bond of 80%.

Before investing in any bond, first, carefully go through its terms and conditions. Read in between the lines and clearly understand the offer. As a general precaution, never invest money you intend to use on emergencies. Ensure you have adequate financial liquidity to sustain you as you wait for the bond to mature. And most significant, keenly analyze the expected performance of the bond during its tenure. You should involve services of a trusted financial advisor, or you can as well carry out the analysis on your own (if you have the relevant know-how).

It's the credit quality of the issuer of a bond which determines the quality of the bond's yield. Mostly, bonds of higher qualities are issued by governments. Equally, companies/institutions linked to governments such as banks also do offer quality bonds. When investing in bonds offered by corporate entities, settle on a bond from good-rated corporate.

## ❖ Invest in unit trusts

A unit trust or unit fund is another favorable investment option offered by several banks, investment banks, other financial institutions, and insurance companies. Your money is pooled together with money from other investors, and thereafter, carefully invested in a portfolio of assets according to the fund's declared investment goals and best fitting investment approaches. In a nutshell, unit trusts are generally managed by experienced fund managers and do operate on a trust structure.

The price of each unit correlates to the fund's net asset value. It's determined by dividing the current market value of the fund's net assets by the number of outstanding units. Your main gain from investing in unit trusts is realized when the prices of the units rises above the initial price you paid. And notably, a good number of unit trusts do pay dividends at certain stipulated times.

The beauty of investing in unit trusts is that it gives you a safer avenue for investing in a diversified range of assets, thus minimizing your risk exposure. It also grants you a secure access to markets or assets which may be more costly if you were to purchase them on your own. If you love to own shares in the stock market, but lack the necessary know-how, you can test out with investing in unit trusts.

And most significant, unit trusts offer you flexible options to choose from. If you want total safety for your invested money, you may settle on unit trusts with capital preservation and income generation. Here, it is the investment banks or insurance companies who bear the risk associated with investing your money. But if you long for more appreciation of your money and you are willing to accept greater risks, then you can settle on funds inclined towards helping your invested money grow.

## ❖ Re-invest in your business

When you feel satisfied with the returns from your business, the least you can do is to plough back all, or part of the profits into the business. By doing so, you are positioning the business for an increased production and more yields. Equally, you can re-invest in the business with the focus of expanding its operations.

## ❖ Be an angel investor

Do you have a keen eye for identifying those startups with possibly good future potential growth and returns? Today, there are endless startups in pursuit of either financial or technical support. You can carefully identify one, invest in it and reap the sweet rewards later after it has stabilized.

## 5. Avoid crowd-guided savings and investment approaches

You must safeguard your savings and investments from avoidable potential losses. Anyway, why would you sacrifice part of your earnings for all those five, ten or twenty years, only to end up losing them in an avoidable unscrupulous deal?

Today, there is a heap of wrong financial advice given by 'financial experts' whose education backgrounds and experiences lie in other fields. Truth is, most financial and investment institutions today are more profit driven, rather than driven by the desire to give their clients value for their money. You must therefore, learn to listen to your instinct as you seek for any savings or investment related advice.

That everyone in your office is excited and rushing towards investing in certain shares should not be an excuse for you to hurriedly invest in those shares as well without any sound financial or investment advice.

## 6. Only get into debt you can afford

You've endlessly heard that *you should never test the depth of a river with both feet.* Do you think you can have a comfortable sleep, or be able to move around peacefully, knowing that you used your car, house, business, or some precious household item as a collateral to a credit facility you've defaulted on, with no possible signs of being able to pay up?

Naturally, borrowing money signifies some "incompleteness" and may literally turn you into a master - if someone owes you, or a slave - if you owe someone. It's a two edged sword. You must therefore, discipline yourself to only borrow money you can comfortably repay. Significantly, learn to only get into debt when you're in need of purchasing items with appreciating values, or for any viable business venture.

For purchase of assets with non-increasing values, you should save towards acquiring them, or purchase them from your income. You must learn to manage your appetite for taking more loans unnecessarily, as such might trap you into the bottomless pit of debt. Well, debt isn't bad, but unplanned debt is like poison to a nicely prepared meal!

7. **Spend more on items offering you savings on purchases**

Why would you want to buy a new television set from a high end retailer when your next door neighbor who is relocating to another country is offering a similar one month old TV for sale at half the original price? And do you really need to take lunch every day at that high end hotel (with highly priced menu) while you have a fridge and a microwave in the office to help you store and heat up that packed lunch from home? And why would you want to sleep out in that fancy hotel when your home/house is just a stone throw away? And strange still, why would you save to purchase a car if you have no urgent use of it? Why would you insist on buying it if you have no adequate money to buy its insurance cover, to fuel it, and or to service it?

8. **Own your dwelling place**

Own where you live. Or any amount you pay towards rent should be geared towards owning that house. Paying rent is a liability, but if the payment of that rent is geared towards owning that house someday, then that's an asset. Owning your place of dwelling will not only offer you convenience, freedom and peace of mind, but will equally help you free that *rent money* to utilize on other projects such as savings, investments and or on any emergent financial need.

9. **Shun the company of negative financial influencers**

Never be afraid of saying NO to unjustifiable financial solicitations, be it from friends, relatives or colleagues. A famous connotation goes; *show me your bank account balance and I will show you your friends.* The world has conditioned us to "hang out" with people within our 'classes'. We consequently end up having friends whose earning and spending abilities are almost commensurate with ours.

But there are some friends and colleagues who will always want to take advantage of your financial innocence and exploit you to their advantage. As an example, they will never hesitate to take you out to the best hotel around for lunch, but end up making you pay all the bills. Equally, they will want to lure you to purchase a personal car to take them out every weekend, while they buy homes whose values keep appreciating each month. While you are focused on pimping that car to match their taste, they on the other hand are working on acquiring a secondary house, or even a parcel of land somewhere.

Hang out with people who respect your wallet. Not those crafty scavengers who retire to bed while scheming on how to 'extract' money from you the next day. Avoid those stingy, night-club-thirsty brokes who can't even buy for themselves drinking water at that fancy night club they frequent courtesy of your wallet. Always remember that there are people who will only be around you when your life is filled with good fortunes, but you'll never see them during your financially trying times.

10. **Never lend money you can't afford to live without**

Lending money to very close friends or relatives, especially to those people who can easily take advantage of your generosity usually have ugly endings.

Truth is it's never easy as an individual to successfully recover money which has fallen in the hands of *a wrong borrower*. It's therefore, essential to arm yourself with the below **six simple safety measures you can adopt to help you lend your money safely**, if you must. Here they are:

&#10003; **Only lend money you are willing to lose**

If you are not willing to lose that money, don't lend it to anyone. If you can't live without that money, don't give it out. It's that simple!

&#10003; **Establish the credit rating/credit score of the borrower**

Technically, most individual lenders would want to shy away from taking this route, but in case you want to guarantee the safety of your money, you should ask the lender to provide you with his credit rating/score, obtained from a reputational credit reference provider. This will help you establish if the borrower has any history of unpaid or defaulted payments.

&#10003; **Know the personal details of the borrower**

Know where the borrower lives, where he/she works, his/her permanent home address, and some of his/her relatives, friends, and even family members you can contact in case he/she defaults or in case he/she is unreachable.

✓ **Ask for a guarantee or a guarantor**

You can ask the borrower to provide you with collateral of a similar or more value for the borrowed amount, or have a reputable individual act as a guarantor to the borrower. In case of any trouble in payment, or total default in payment, this will help you to know where to turn to.

✓ **Keep an updated track of the borrower**

You can occasionally call the borrower just to get to know how he/she is fairing on. You can equally occasionally call the guarantor, if any, to ascertain the wellbeing of the borrower.

✓ **And why not insure that money?**

Practically, this might not be possible in several countries due to unavailability of relevant covers. Designing appropriate insurance covers for individual money lenders is literally an underwriting headache to many insurance companies. But if you come across such relevant insurance covers, which can shield you against losing the money you are lending, then never hesitate to grab such covers.

## 11. Have an emergency kitty

An emergency kitty will always shield you from viewing credit as your safety net. And in the event of exposure to unavoidable life's emergencies or tragedies such as sickness, job loss, or even death, you'll always have somewhere to turn to for financial help.

12. **Take good care of your health**

Most probably, you've heard that your health is your wealth. Go for those periodical checkups, eat healthy foods and on diet, drink lots of water, meditate often, and do regular exercises. Do whatever you can to stay healthy all the time. And whatever strategies you adopt to help you acquire more money, ensure your health is never put at risk. After all, what would be the essence of acquiring all that wealth, only to lose your life the next morning on avoidable health-related grounds?

13. **Always give back**

You will never lack by giving. As a sign of gratitude, always give something to those less fortunate members of the society (those who may never be in any position to pay you back). What special talent do you have? Can you find some time to mentor others? Use that unique gift you have to lift up or encourage someone else. The biggest secret to being alive is in giving back. Give freely, as much as you possibly can.